BUNNY MAN BRIDGE

This series features unsolved mysteries, urban legends, and other curious stories. Each creepy, shocking, or befuddling book focuses on what people believe and hear. True or not? That's for you to decide!

45th Parallel Press

Published in the United States of America by Cherry Lake Publishing
Ann Arbor, Michigan
www.cherrylakepublishing.com

Reading Adviser: Marla Conn MS, Ed., Literacy specialist, Read-Ability, Inc.
Book Designer: Felicia Macheske

Photo Credits: © Jaromir Chalabala/Shutterstock.com, cover; © Evannovostro/Shutterstock.com, 5;
© StockLite/Shutterstock.com, 7; © Quorthon1/Shutterstock.com, 8; © IDostal/Shutterstock.com, 11;
© Photographee.eu/Shutterstock.com, 12; © Romolo Tavani/Shutterstock.com, 15; © powerofforever/iStock.
com, 17; © GI0ck/Shutterstock.com, 18; © katalinks/Shutterstock.com, 20; © IPK Photography/Shutterstock.
com, 23; © Jeffrey M. Frank/Shutterstock.com, 24; © rangizzz/Shutterstock.com, 27; © Laurin Rinder/
Shutterstock.com, 29

Graphic Elements Throughout: © iofoto/Shutterstock.com; © COLCU/Shutterstock.com; © spacedrone808/
Shutterstock.com; © rf.vector.stock/Shutterstock.com; © donatas1205/Shutterstock.com; © cluckva/
Shutterstock.com; © Eky Studio/Shutterstock.com

45th Parallel Press is an imprint of Cherry Lake Publishing.

Library of Congress Cataloging-in-Publication Data has been filed and is available at catalog.loc.gov

Cherry Lake Publishing would like to acknowledge the work of The Partnership for 21st Century Skills.
Please visit *www.p21.org* for more information.

Printed in the United States of America
Corporate Graphics

TABLE OF CONTENTS

Chapter One

HAUNTED TUNNEL OF FEAR

What did Angie Proffitt see? What are the rumors about Bunny Man Bridge? What do teens do at Bunny Man Bridge?

Angie Proffitt visited Bunny Man Bridge. She'll never forget what happened. She was 14 years old. It was in the 1970s. Her boyfriend wanted to scare her. They went to a dark tunnel. The tunnel was under a railroad bridge. It was at a dead-end road. It was dark. They parked near the bridge.

Proffitt believes she saw two children. The children were at the tunnel opening. Suddenly, they disappeared. Then, they were at the back window of the car. They were looking right at Proffitt. Proffitt said, "Those children were **victims**. They died there." Victims are targets of crimes.

People see ghosts at Bunny Man Bridge.

CONSIDER THE
EVIDENCE

Criminals do bad things. They break laws. They wear disguises. They want to hide their appearance. They want to change how they look. They don't want people to know who they are. They don't want to get caught. They don't want to go to prison. Bank robbers have worn ski masks. They've worn dark sunglasses. They've worn knit caps. They've worn panty hose on their heads. The greater the change, the harder it is to be identified. Changes in hairstyles affect identification. Changes in facial hair affect identification. Addition or removal of glasses affects identification. A bunny man costume seems to hide everything. Doesn't it?

There are many **rumors** about Bunny Man Bridge. Rumors are stories. People doubt they're true. But they believe some parts. These are some rumors:

- A man dressed like a bunny. He killed his family. He hung himself on the bridge.
- A killer wore a bunny suit. He attacked people who came to the bridge. He used an ax.
- A man lived alone. He killed two children. Teens went to the bridge. They found their bodies.
- It was Halloween. Three teens were killed. They were found hanging from the bridge. There was a note at their feet. It read, "You'll never catch the Bunny Man."

The U.S. is filled with haunted bridges, houses, and other buildings.

People believe over 30 deaths happened at the bridge.

These stories excite teens. Many teens visit Bunny Man Bridge. They want a good scare. They go at night. They look for the Bunny Man.

In 2001, six teens searched the area. They found cut-up bunny parts. They heard noises. They saw movement in the woods. They ran away.

Some teens are extreme. They go to the bridge at midnight on Halloween. It's believed that doing so means death! Teens stand in the tunnel. They say, "Bunny Man." They say this three times. This makes Bunny Man appear.

Chapter Two

FEAR THE BUNNY MAN

What is the legend of the Bunny Man?
Who is Douglas J. Grifon?

Bunny Man is an **urban legend**. Urban legends are modern folktales. Many people have told this story.

The story takes place in Clifton, Virginia. It starts in the early 1900s. There was a nearby **asylum** for the criminally insane. This is a home for crazy criminals. It was shut down. The criminals were taken to a new place. They were put on a bus. The bus crashed. It crashed at the bridge. Most people died.

Two criminals escaped. Their names were Marcus Wallster and Douglas J. Grifon. These two were the most dangerous. They hid in the woods.

People say they see Bunny Man. He stands in the shadows. He waits.

Police search for dangerous criminals.

They ate rabbits to stay alive. Hundreds of rabbit parts were found. The rabbits were skinned. They were half-eaten. They were hanging from trees.

Cops looked for the criminals. They looked for months. They found Wallster. Wallster was hanging from the bridge. He looked like the hanging rabbits.

Cops accused Grifon of killing Wallster. They called Grifon "Bunny Man." Bunny Man was hard to find. But the cops finally found him. They found him at the bridge. They almost lost him. But then a train hit him. They thought Bunny Man died. But the cops never found his body. This happened on Halloween.

SPOTLIGHT
BIOGRAPHY

Donna DeSoto lives in Fairfax. She makes quilts. She belongs to Quilters Unlimited. This group issued a challenge. Members were asked to make quilts. The theme was "Virginia's beautiful waters." DeSoto was inspired by the brooks in Clifton's woods. She made a quilt about Bunny Man. She said, "You can't depict the woods in Clifton without thinking about the Bunny Man Bridge." She sewed little silver skulls on the bottom of the quilt. She wanted to add tiny hatchets. The quilt is named "Eek from the Creek: Encounter with Clifton's Bunny Man." She used a Big Foot pattern to make the Bunny Man.

Cops heard him laughing. They learned Bunny Man had killed his family on Easter Sunday. That is why he was in prison in the first place.

Bunny Man's ghost haunts the bridge on Halloween. He does this around midnight. He wears a bunny suit. He kills people who walk through the tunnel. He chases victims with an ax. He grabs them from behind. He hangs them from the bridge. He cuts people open. He takes out their organs.

He gives warnings. He hangs rabbits from the bridge. He throws axes at cars' back windows. He does this right before Halloween.

Halloween opens doorways between this world and other worlds.

Chapter Three

PROOF OF AN EVIL BUNNY?

Who's Brian A. Conley? What happened to Bob Bennett? What happened to Paul Phillips?

Brian A. Conley is a historian. He works at Fairfax County Public Library. This is close to Clifton. He studies the Bunny Man legend. He is a Bunny Man expert. He confirmed two events that support Bunny Man. Twice, a man in a bunny suit carrying an ax was spotted. These events happened in 1970. They happened a week apart. These events may have inspired the Bunny Man legend.

Cops investigated. They didn't find the man in a bunny suit. There wasn't enough proof. But over 50 people called the cops. They reported seeing the "Bunny Man."

Every legend has some truth to it.

Some say Bunny Man smashes car windows with an ax.

The first event happened on October 19, 1970. Bob Bennett was a U.S. Air Force Academy **cadet**. Cadets are students. Bennett was visiting family. He was near Clifton. He went to a football game. He took his girlfriend. They left the game. They parked by the bridge.

Bennett saw a man. The man wore a white suit. He wore long bunny ears. He smashed the front window. He yelled, "You're on private property." Bennett drove away. Later he found an ax on the car floor. He told the cops.

REAL-WORLD
CONNECTION

A big white rabbit lives in Barnes. Barnes is in South West London. The rabbit is over 6 feet (2 meters) tall. He wears a colorful waistcoat. He wears a colorful scarf. He sits by the Thames River. He dances around. He waves at cars. He waves a heart. The heart is cut out from paper. It has glitter. He does this on the first day of each month. He started doing this in November 2015. He wants to delight people. He wants to take people's minds off bad news. But some people think he's creepy. The rabbit is really Spike McLarrity. McLarrity is a performance artist.

The man was called the Rabbit of Guinea Road.

The second event happened on October 29, 1970. Paul Phillips was a security guard. He worked on a construction site. He was near Clifton. He saw a man. The man was on the porch of an unfinished house. He wore a white bunny suit. He was about 20 years old. He was 5 feet and 8 inches (173 centimeters) tall. He weighed about 175 pounds (79 kilograms). He chopped at a post. He used an ax. He said, "All you people **trespass** around here. If you don't get out of here, I'm going to bust you on the head." Trespass means to be on someone else's land. Phillips told the cops.

Chapter Four

CREEPY CLIFTON

What is the history of Bunny Man Bridge?
Why is Clifton scary?

Clifton is a city in northern Virginia. It's in Fairfax County. This is close to Washington, D.C. Washington, D.C. is our nation's capital. Bunny Man Bridge is in Clifton. It's on Colchester Road. This road is narrow. It's curvy. It's hard to see things. It can be a dangerous road.

Bunny Man Bridge's real name is Colchester **Overpass**. An overpass is a special bridge. Roads or railroads pass over it. Bunny Man Bridge is really a concrete tunnel. It's one lane. It's painted white. It's about 20 feet (6 m) long. It's under a railroad track. Ninety trains use it each week.

The bridge is sometimes called the Clifton Overpass.

Clifton was known as Devereux Station. It was a railroad station. The station turned Clifton into a town. It was built during the Civil War. The Civil War happened in the 1860s. The North fought the South. Many battles were fought near Clifton. The most famous battle was Bull Run. Many people died. Some people think Clifton is haunted. They see ghosts. They see dead soldiers. Now, they see Bunny Man. Bunny Man Bridge was built in 1906.

Clifton was a farming community.

INVESTIGATION TIPS

- Talk to people who live in northern Virginia. Talk to people who live in Clifton, Virginia. Ask them if they went to Bunny Man Bridge.

- Attend the Clifton Haunted Trail. This happens in October. Buy tickets. Wear good shoes. Prepare to be scared.

- Go to the Fairfax County Public Library. Learn more about Bunny Man Bridge.

- Read local newspapers from northern Virginia. Check out the crime reports. Look for unusual crimes around Bunny Man Bridge.

- Go to Bunny Man Bridge. Stay in the car. Keep the car running. Don't stop. Don't park. Don't go at night.

Chapter Five

BUNNY MAN BUSTED!

What are sightings? What are the problems with the Bunny Man legend?

Sightings are reports. Bunny Man sightings are popular in Clifton. But people have seen him in other places. They've seen him in Fairfax County. They've seen him in Maryland. They've seen him in D.C. People see him chasing children with axes. They see him attacking adults in their cars. They see him destroying property.

Sightings aren't **reliable**. This means they can't be trusted. People believe what they want. Something happened. But it might not be the Bunny Man. People know the story. So, they refer to it. They recall details. They think they're telling the truth.

Bunny Man hangs around northern Virginia.

EXPLAINED BY SCIENCE

Bridges let people travel over water and gaps. Engineers study how bridges work. They make bridges safe. They consider spans, or distances. They consider weight. This is load. Load depends on what crosses bridges. Forces push. Forces pull. Engineers balance these forces. They make bridges stay in place. Load causes forces. Some forces press down. Some forces stretch out. Too much force in one area is bad. Bridges fall down. Engineers design bridges to move forces around. They spread out forces. They move forces from weak to strong spots. Bridge decks need support. They carry heavy loads. Engineers use beams, arches, trusses, and suspensions.

There are problems with the Bunny Man story. First, there's no asylum. City records show no place existed. Second, the criminals were being taken to Lorton Prison. But this can't be true. Lorton wasn't built yet. Lorton wasn't part of Virginia. It was part of D.C. Third, Grifon and Wallster don't exist. No court records of them can be found. Fourth, there aren't records of deaths around the bridge.

Real or not? It doesn't matter. The Bunny Man lives in people's imaginations.

Urban legends are scary stories. But people say they're based in truth.

DID YOU KNOW?

- There's a band called Bunny Man Bridge. It plays funk. It plays jazz. It plays R&B. It's based in northern Virginia. It was formed in 2014.

- People live in Clifton, Virginia. They don't like teens going to the bridge late at night. This is disruptive. They don't like teens painting graffiti on the bridge.

- Ivakota Farm was in Clifton, Virginia. It housed unwed mothers and their children. This turned into a local urban legend. Some people believe the Bunny Man killed the girls. Their ghosts haunt the area.

- President Jimmy Carter was fishing. A swamp rabbit came to his boat. Carter used a paddle. He splashed water at the rabbit. People say he got attacked by a killer rabbit. This happened in 1979.

- The Killer Rabbit of Caerbannog is from a movie. The movie is *Monty Python and the Holy Grail*. The Killer Rabbit is the guardian of the Black Beast of Aaaaarrrrrggghhh.

- The White Rabbit is from *Alice's Adventures in Wonderland*. It's the first Wonderland character Alice meets. It's famous for being late.

- *Donnie Darko* is a 2001 movie. Darko is a troubled teen. He sees a rabbit named Frank. Frank is evil. Richard Kelly is the writer and director. Kelly is from Virginia.

CONSIDER THIS!

Take a Position: You read that people in Clifton, Virginia, don't like teens going to Bunny Man Bridge. Should it be closed off to the public? Argue your point with reasons and evidence.

Say What? Read the 45th Parallel books about Bloody Mary and Hookman. Explain how these stories are alike. Explain how they are different. Which story do you like the best? Explain why.

Think About It! Many teenagers visit Bunny Man Bridge. Why do teens go there? Would you go? Why or why not?

LEARN MORE

- Latham, Donna, and Jen Vaughn (illustrator). *Bridges and Tunnels: Investigate Feats of Engineering*. White River Junction, VT: Nomad Press, 2012.

- Loh-Hagan, Virginia. *Bridges*. Ann Arbor, MI: Cherry Lake Publishing, 2017.

- Schwartz, Alvin. *Scary Stories to Tell in the Dark*. New York: HarperCollins Publishers, 2005.

- Young, Richard, and Judy Dockrey Young. *Favorite Scary Stories of American Children*. Little Rock, AR: August House, 1999.

GLOSSARY

asylum (uh-SYE-luhm) institution, hospital, care facility

cadet (kuh-DET) student, trainee

overpass (OH-vur-pas) a bridge on which a road or railroad passes over

reliable (rih-LYE-uh-buhl) trustworthy

rumors (ROO-mur) gossip; stories that may or may not be true

sightings (SITE-ingz) reports of seeing something

trespass (TRES-pas) to be on someone else's property

urban legend (UR-buhn LEJ-uhnd) modern folktale

victims (VIK-tuhmz) targets of crime

INDEX

ABOUT THE AUTHOR

Dr. Virginia Loh-Hagan is an author, university professor, former classroom teacher, and curriculum designer. She was born and raised in Fairfax, Virginia. She remembers going to Bunny Man Bridge as a teenager. She lives in San Diego with her very tall husband and very naughty dogs. To learn more about her, visit www.virginialoh.com.